FROM THE HANDS OF A CHILD II

Three-Dimensional Art Activities for Primary Children

by Anthony Flores

D1517469

Fearon Teacher Aids

A Paramount Communications Company

Editorial Director: Virginia L. Murphy
Editor: Carolea Williams
Copyeditor: Kristin Eclov
Cover Design: Teena Remer
Inside Design: Walt Shelly
Inside Illustration: Janet Skiles
Production: Rebecca Speakes

ISBN 0-86653-917-4

Printed in the United States of America
1. 9 8 7 6

Contents

Contents

Introduction

From the Hands of a Child II provides you with art lessons that are unique for each child. As in many art activity books, the lessons are seasonal by month. Yet each of these three-dimensional activities is special because it incorporates the hand tracings of each individual child.

Lessons include teacher's notes and reproducible pattern pages. The activity directions are printed on the pattern pages and are an excellent resource for practice in reading and reinforcing skills in following directions. With these art projects, children will practice cutting various shapes, arranging paper pieces to create sculptures and other three-dimensional objects. The projects also offer practice with color and shape recognition and with spatial awareness.

The color combinations indicated are not required. You may want to invite children to choose other colors than those listed in the lessons. The necessary materials for each art project are listed in the teacher's notes. Encourage the children to add their own ideas.

General Directions for All Projects

Each project begins with a base for creating the sculpture or three-dimensional project. Bases include stuffed paper bags, lanterns, and cylinders. Each child creates the base before beginning the next steps of each project.

Duplicate the pattern pages on heavy paper, which is easier for young children to cut. Provide box lids so that each student may keep his or her pattern pieces at hand during the art lesson. (Small pattern pieces are apt to fly off the desk and get lost.)

Distribute the required materials. Ask the students to read the directions on the pattern page with you. Explain the symbols in the directions. ✏ means to draw, trace, or write. ✂ means to cut and 🖌 means to paste. Young children or developmentally disadvantaged children who cannot read can also successfully complete the projects independently using the direction symbols, the pictures of the pattern pieces, and the sample of the completed project.

Demonstrate the best ways of tracing the children's hands. Show the students how to fold construction paper in half and how to place patterns on the folds efficiently. With primary students, make sure they understand the directions thoroughly before they proceed with the lesson. Capable second- or third-graders, however, may be able to complete some of these art projects independently without initial guidance.

The fourth project for each month is a bulletin-board display. Teacher's notes include suggestions for background colors and helpful hints for making the display attractive.

September

Paper-Bag Portraits

Materials for each child:
- brown, yellow, black, blue, red, and green construction paper
- paper bag
- scrap paper or crumpled newspaper
- stapler
- markers or crayons
- scissors and paste

Encourage students to be imaginative as they create different hats and facial expressions for their paper-bag portraits.

Paper-Bag House

Materials for each child:
- brown, green, red, and white, construction paper
- paper bag
- scrap paper or crumpled newspaper
- stapler
- markers or crayons
- pattern page
- scissors and paste

Discuss features of a house, such as doors, windows, roofs, and chimneys. Invite children to place their finished houses on a large piece of green butcher paper to make a community or neighborhood. Add streets and other details.

Basket Full of Good Apples

Materials for each child:
- red and green construction paper
- markers or crayons
- pattern page
- scissors and paste

Place students' name apples in a large basket. Pull apples out of the basket to choose monitors, helpers, or cooperative groups. Or, designate a special basket to honor students. For example, place the apples of students who did well on their spelling tests in a "good spelling basket."

Our Class Tree

Materials for each child:
- red, yellow, orange, or brown construction paper
- markers or crayons
- scissors and paste

Cover a bulletin board with blue butcher paper. Create a tree using crumpled grocery bags and a stapler. Place as many branches on the tree as there are cooperative groups in the class. Add a simple fall border. Cut out letters to make the display heading **Our Class Tree.**

This is a good project for building self esteem at the beginning of school. Each child writes his or her name on a fall leaf. Each branch represents a cooperative group with the hands of the children in that group stapled to the branch.

Paper-Bag Portraits

1. Stuff a ⬜ with scrap paper or crumpled newspaper.

2. Staple it closed across the top.

3. ✏️ around many 🖐 on paper the color of your hair.

4. ✂️ them out.

5. 🫙 them to the top and sides of the stuffed bag to make hair.

6. ✂️ features from colored scraps of paper using the feature patterns on page 96.

7. 🫙 features to the stuffed bag.

8. You may want to ✏️ features on your stuffed bag using markers or crayons instead of cutting them from paper.

9. ✂️ out a creative hat from paper using the ideas on page 9.

10. 🫙 the hat on top of the paper-bag head.

From the Hands of a Child II © 1994 Fearon Teacher Aids

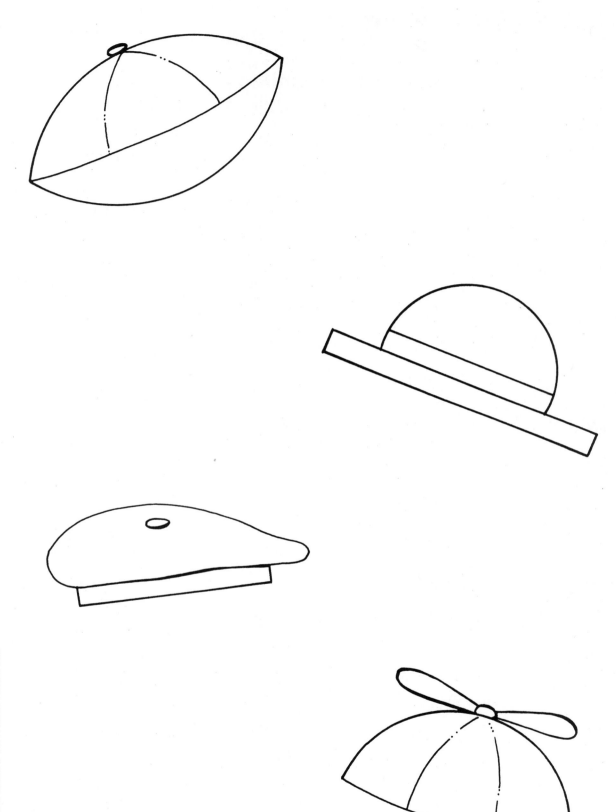

Paper-Bag House

1. Stuff a  with scrap paper or crumpled newspaper.

2. Staple it closed across the top.

3. ✏️ around many 🖐️ on red or brown paper.

4. ✂️ them out.

5. 🧴 them to the top third of the ⌂.

6. ✂️ out the ☐ ▯ ▭.

7. ✏️ around the ▯ on brown paper.

8. ✂️ it out.

9. ✏️ around the ☐ on white paper.

10. ✂️ it out.

11. ✏️ a 🚪 and ⊞ using markers or crayons.

12. ✂️ them out.

13. 🧴 them on the ⌂.

14. ✏️ around many 🖐️ on green paper.

15. ✂️ them out.

16. ✏️ around many ▭ on brown paper.

17. ✂️ them out.

18. 🧴 1 green 🖐️ to each brown ▭.

19. Place your 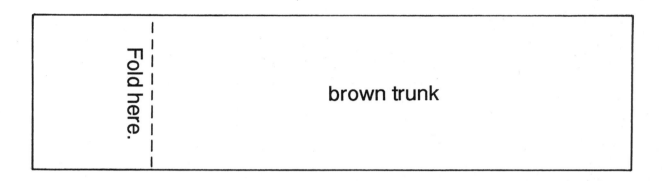 on a table covered with green butcher

paper.

20. Bend the bottom of each ✍🏻⊐ and 🗲 the tab to the green

paper around your 🏠 .

Fold here.	brown trunk

brown door ○	white window

Basket Full of Good Apples _____

1. ✂ out the 🍎 ⬜ .

2. ✏ 2 🍎🍎 on red paper.

3. ✂ them out.

4. Place 1 🍎 exactly on top of the other 🍎 .

5. 🖌 the edges of the 🍎 . Leave about a 2" (5.0 cm) opening.

6. Stuff the 🍎 with scraps of paper.

7. 🖌 the 2" (5.0 cm) opening closed.

8. ✏ the ⬜ on green paper.

9. ✂ it out.

10. 🖌 the ⬜ to the top of the 🍎 .

11. ✏ around 1 ✋ on green paper.

12. ✂ it out.

13. 🖌 it to the top of the 🍎 .

14. ✏ your name on the 🍎 .

_ _

Our Class Tree

1. ✏️ around 1 ✋ on red, yellow, orange, or brown paper.

2. ✂️ it out.

3. ✏️ your name on your ✋ with a marker or crayon.

4. Ask your teacher to staple your ✋ to the bulletin-board tree.

green stem

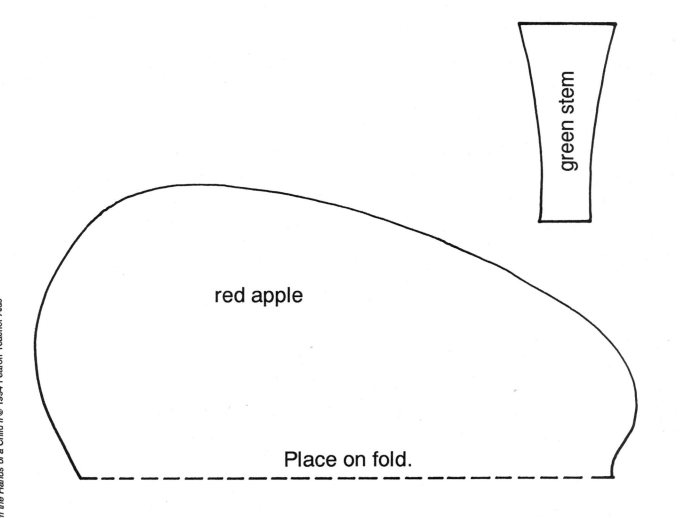

red apple

Place on fold.

October

Jack-O'-Lantern

Materials for each child:
- orange, black, and green construction paper
- ruler
- pattern page
- scissors and paste

This page provides practice in drawing and cutting out small geometric shapes.

   Cover a table top with green butcher paper and encourage children to place their finished lanterns on it.

Paper-Bag Scarecrow

Materials for each child:
- black, orange, light brown, yellow, red, and white construction paper
- paper bag
- scrap paper or crumpled newspaper
- stapler
- markers or crayons
- pattern page
- scissors and paste

Discuss the purpose of a scarecrow. Ask the children where they might find a scarecrow. Encourage children to be creative when making hats for their scarecrows.

Cylinder Owl

Materials for each child:
- brown, orange, white, and black construction paper
- ruler
- pattern page
- scissors and paste

The owl is a very interesting animal to study. Invite the children to read about owls and make a list of special features that make this bird unique.

As children make this project, point out the symmetry in the placement of the wings and eyes.

Ghostly Figures

Materials for each child:
- black, white, and green construction paper
- scissors and paste

Cover a bulletin board with black butcher paper. Create a grass base using green hand tracings that the children make. Cut out letters to make the display heading **Ghostly Figures.**

Divide the class into small cooperative groups to work on this project. Each group can create a ghostly figure.

Jack-O'-Lantern ———————————————

1. Fold a 9" x 12" (22.9 cm x 30.5 cm) sheet of orange construction paper in half. ⬭

2. ✏ a line across the open edge 1 1/2" (3.9 cm) from the top. ⬭

3. ✏ lines 1" (2.5 cm) apart from the folded edge up to the pencil line. ⬭

4. ✂ the lines from the fold up to the pencil line.

5. Unfold and roll into a cylinder shape. ◫

6. 🖋 edges in place.

7. ✏ around 1 ✋ on green paper.

8. ✂ it out.

9. 🖋 it to the top of the lantern.

10. ✂ out the △ △ ○ ▭ .

11. ✏ △ △ ○ ▭ on black paper.

12. ✂ them out.

13. 🖋 the ⏢ to the front of the lantern.

From the Hands of a Child II © 1994 Fearon Teacher Aids

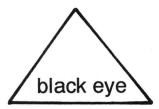
black eye

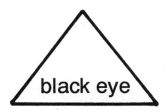
black eye

black nose

black mouth

Paper-Bag Scarecrow

1. Stuff a [bag] with scrap paper or crumpled newspaper.

2. Staple it closed across the top. [bag]

3. [pencil] around many [hand] on yellow construction paper.

4. [scissors] them out.

5. [glue] them to the top and sides of the stuffed bag to make hair.

6. [scissors] features from colored scraps of paper using the feature patterns on page 19.

7. [glue] features to the stuffed bag.

8. You may want to [pencil] features on the stuffed bag using markers or crayons instead of [scissors] them from paper.

9. [pencil] stitch lines down the side of the stuffed bag.

10. [scissors] and [glue] a hat from construction paper. Be creative!

eyes

noses

mouths

  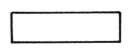 

Cylinder Owl _____

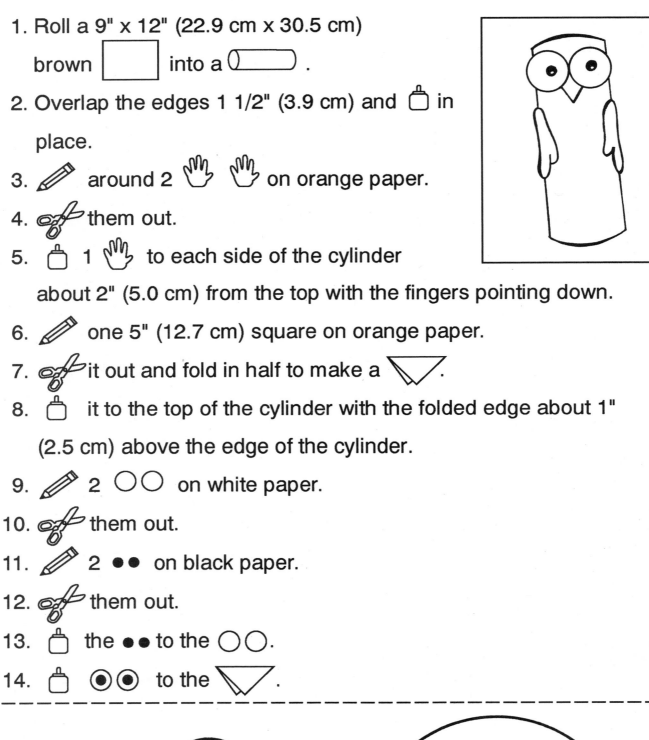

1. Roll a 9" x 12" (22.9 cm x 30.5 cm) brown ▭ into a ⬭ .

2. Overlap the edges 1 1/2" (3.9 cm) and 🖉 in place.

3. ✏ around 2 ✋ ✋ on orange paper.

4. ✂ them out.

5. 🖉 1 ✋ to each side of the cylinder about 2" (5.0 cm) from the top with the fingers pointing down.

6. ✏ one 5" (12.7 cm) square on orange paper.

7. ✂ it out and fold in half to make a ◺ .

8. 🖉 it to the top of the cylinder with the folded edge about 1" (2.5 cm) above the edge of the cylinder.

9. ✏ 2 ⬯⬯ on white paper.

10. ✂ them out.

11. ✏ 2 ●● on black paper.

12. ✂ them out.

13. 🖉 the ●● to the ⬯⬯ .

14. 🖉 ◉◉ to the ◺ .

- -

black
pupil

white eye

Place on fold.

Ghostly Figures

1. ✏️ around 3 ✋ ✋ ✋ on green paper.

2. ✂️ them out.

3. Ask your teacher to staple them to the bulletin board.

4. In your group, ✏️ many ✋ on white paper.

5. ✂️ them out.

6. Ask your teacher to staple them to the bulletin board to make a ghostly creature.

7. ✂️ features from black paper.

8. 🖋️ them to your ghost figures.

GHOSTLY FIGURES

November

Turkey Sculpture

Materials for each child:
- orange, brown, yellow, and red construction paper
- paper bag
- scrap paper or crumpled newspaper
- stapler
- markers or crayons
- pattern page
- scissors and paste

When explaining placement of features and feathers use words, such as *middle, behind, above, beside,* and *under.* Encourage children to artistically plan how they will arrange the hand tracings to make a creative turkey tail. Children can make a color pattern, such as yellow, red, orange, yellow, red, orange.

Native American Sculptures

Materials for each child:
- black, orange, light brown, yellow, red, and white construction paper
- paper bag
- scrap paper or crumpled newspaper
- stapler
- markers or crayons
- pattern page
- scissors and paste

Discuss the first meeting between the Pilgrims and the Native Americans. Invite children to discuss some of the many contributions Native Americans have made to this country. Be sure children are aware that one style of dress does not typify the entire Native American population. Challenge children to research various tribes and customs.

Pilgrim Sculptures

Materials for each child:
- black, brown, yellow, orange, and white construction paper
- paper bag
- scrap paper or crumpled newspaper
- stapler
- markers or crayons
- pattern page
- scissors and paste

This project also follows the discussion mentioned in the previous lesson. Instead of all the children making Native Americans, have half make Pilgrims.

We Are Thankful

Materials for each child:
- green, red, yellow, and orange construction paper
- markers or crayons
- scissors

Cover a bulletin board with black butcher paper. Accordion pleat four 18" x 22" (45.7 cm x 55 cm) pieces of tissue paper (red, orange, brown, and yellow). Stack one on top of the other and staple in the center. Pull up one sheet at a time to fluff into a large flower shape. Staple it to the center of the bulletin board to make a turkey body. Enlarge the turkey patterns on page 29 and cut them out. Trace the head on brown paper, the waddle on red paper, and the beak and feet on yellow paper. Cut them out and staple in place on the bulletin board. Cut out letters to make the display heading **We Are Thankful.**

Turkey Sculpture

1. Stuff a ▯ with scrap paper or crumpled newspaper.

2. Staple it closed across the top. ▱

3. ✏ around many ✋ on orange, brown, red, and yellow paper.

4. ✂ them out.

5. 🖊 2 ✋ ✋ to the front of both sides of the stuffed bag to make wings.

6. 🖊 2 rows of ✋ to the top back of the stuffed bag to make a tail.

7. ✏ the ⬭ on orange paper.

8. ✂ it out.

9. 🖊 it to the center front of the stuffed bag.

10. ✏ an eye on the ⬭. Color the waddle red.

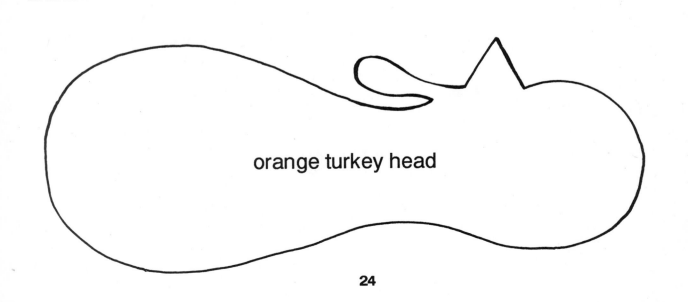

orange turkey head

From the Hands of a Child II © 1994 Fearon Teacher Aids

Native American Sculptures ___

1. Stuff a ⬜ with scrap paper or crumpled newspaper.

2. Staple it closed across the top. 🛍️

3. ✏️ around many ✋ on black paper.

4. ✂️ them out.

5. 🧴 them to the top and sides of the stuffed bag to make hair.

6. ✂️ features from colored scraps of paper using the feature patterns on page 96.

7. 🧴 features to the stuffed bag.

8. You many want to ✏️ features on the stuffed bag using markers or crayons instead of ✂️ them from paper.

From the Hands of a Child II © 1994 Fearon Teacher Aids

Pilgrim Sculptures

1. Stuff a ⬜ with scrap paper or crumpled newspaper.

2. Staple it closed across the top.

3. ✏️ around many ✋ on black, brown, or yellow paper.

4. ✂️ them out.

5. 🖊️ the ✋ to the top and sides of the stuffed bag to make hair.

6. ✂️ features from colored scraps of paper using the feature patterns on page 96.

7. 🖊️ features to the stuffed bag.

8. You may want to ✏️ features on the stuffed bag using markers or crayons instead of ✂️ them from paper.

9. ✏️ the ⬛ on black paper or the ⬜ on white paper.

10. ✂️ out the ⬛ ⬜ .

11. 🖊️ the ⬛ to the top of the stuffed bag.

From the Hands of a Child II © 1994 Fearon Teacher Aids

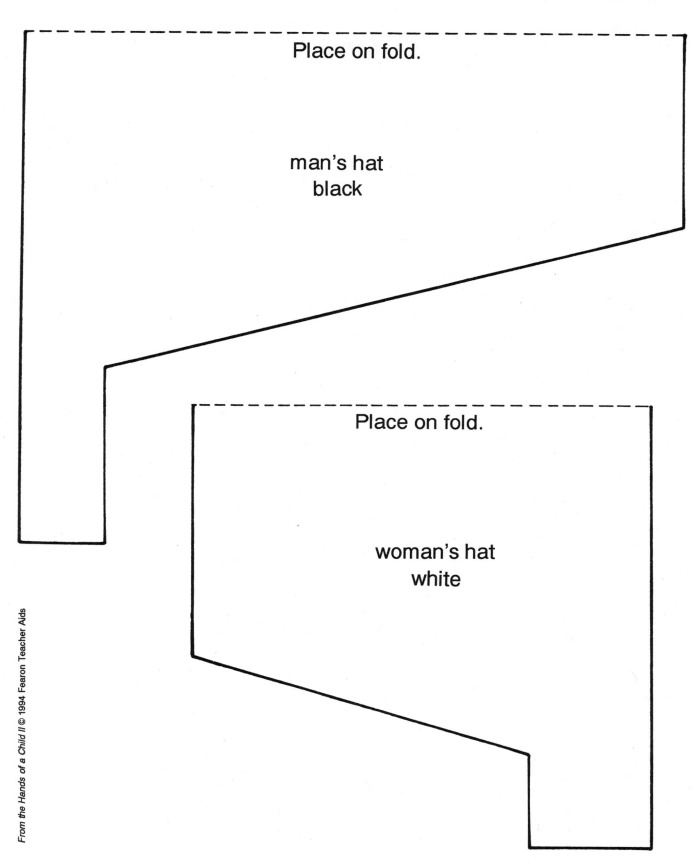

Place on fold.

man's hat
black

Place on fold.

woman's hat
white

We Are Thankful _____

1. ✏️ around 2 🖐️ 🖐️ on green paper.

2. ✂️ them out.

3. Ask your teacher to staple them to the bottom of the bulletin board to make grass.

4. ✏️ around 1 🖐️ on red paper.

5. ✏️ around 1 🖐️ on yellow paper.

6. ✏️ around 1 🖐️ on orange paper.

7. ✂️ them out.

8. Write something you are thankful for on each 🖐️.

9. Ask your teacher to staple the 🖐️ to the bulletin board to make turkey feathers.

WE ARE THANKFUL

From the Hands of a Child II © 1994 Fearon Teacher Aids

yellow beak

yellow leg

red waddle

brown turkey head

December

Cylinder Santa

Materials for each child:
- white, red, pink, brown, and green construction paper
- black marker
- pattern page
- scissors and paste

This page provides practice drawing and cutting out small shapes. This is an excellent project for following directions. You may want to enlist some extra volunteer help and give the children an opportunity to work in small groups to complete this project.

Reindeer Bag

Materials for each child:
- black, brown, yellow, red, and white construction paper
- large paper bag
- pattern page
- scissors and paste

Vacation time is a great opportunity to encourage children to clean out their desks. Invite children to carry home their belongings in this festive bag.

Point out the antlers on the reindeer. Encourage children to make a list of other animals that have antlers and to discuss their purposes.

Christmas Angel

Materials for each child:
- brown, pink, white, yellow, green, and black construction paper
- paper bag
- scrap paper or crumpled newspaper
- stapler
- markers or crayons
- pattern page
- scissors and paste

Encourage students to discuss the qualities of an angel. Ask children what similar qualities they notice in themselves or people around them.

The Perfect Gift

Materials for each child:
- green and white construction paper
- markers or crayons
- scissors

Cover a bulletin board with yellow butcher paper. Add a simple Christmas border. Cut out letters to make the display heading **The Perfect Gift.** After children trace their hands, staple them to the bulletin board to create a Christmas tree. Begin with a wide row across the bottom (fingers hanging down) and continue adding rows building towards the top. Each row will be slightly shorter than the one below it. Cut a star from yellow construction using the pattern on page 41. Add it to the top of the tree.

Cylinder Santa

1. Roll a 9" x 12" (22.9 cm x 30.5 cm) red 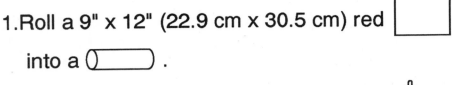 into a ⬭ .

2. Overlap the edges 1 1/2" (3.9 cm) and 🖊 in place.

3. ✂ out the ◯ ○ ⌓ 〰 ⬭ ▯  👍 △ ▭ ○ .

4. ✏ the ◯ on pink or brown paper.

5. ✂ it out.

6. 🖊 the ◯ to the top of the cylinder.

7. ✏ around 2 ✋ ✋ on white paper.

8. ✂ them out.

9. 🖊 1 ✋ to the bottom of the ◯ with the fingers pointing down to make a beard.

10. Curl the fingers to fluff the beard.

11. Fold the palm part of the other ✋ over the back of the 🖐 to make hair.

12. 🖊 it down and curl the fingers.

13. ✏ the △ on red paper.

14. ✂ it out.

15. 🖊 the △ above the curled fingers at the top of the 🖐 .

16. ✏️ the ◯ ⬜ on white paper.

17. ✂️ them out.

18. 🖊️ the ◯ to the top of the 🎅.

19. 🖊️ the ⬜ to the bottom of the 🎅.

20. ✏️ the ⌒ △ ◠ on white paper.

21. ✂️ them out.

22. 🖊️ to the 🎅.

23. ✏️ the ◯ on red paper.

24. ✂️ it out.

25. 🖊️ it above the ⌒.

26. ✏️ a pupil in the center of each 👁️ 👁️ and ✏️ a ‿.

27. ✏️ 2 ▢ ▢ on red paper.

28. ✂️ them out.

29. ✏️ 2 ▷ ▷ on green paper.

30. ✏️ them out.

31. 🖊️ the ▷ to the ends of the ▢.

32. 🖊️ the ▢▷ onto the sides of the cylinder.

33. ✏️ 2 ◫◫ on white paper.

34. ✂️ them out.

35. 🖊️ the ◫ to the ▢▷.

red arm

pink or brown face

red nose

white eye

white moustache

white cuff

red hat

white hat band

green glove

white hat tassel

Reindeer Bag

1. Fold a 9" (22.9 cm) square of brown paper into a ◺.

2. ✏️ around 2 🖐 🖐 on yellow paper.

3. ✂️ them out.

4. 🔾 them to the back of the folded edge of the ◺ to make antlers.

5. ✏️ the ○ on red paper.

6. ✂️ it out.

7. 🔾 it to the bottom of the ◺.

8. ✏️ 2 ○ ○ on white paper.

9. ✂️ them out.

10. ✏️ 2 ○ ○ on black paper.

11. ✂️ them out.

12. 🔾 the • • to the ○ ○ .

13. 🔾 the ◉ ◉ on the ◺.

14. 🔾 the ◺ to the top of a large grocery bag.

15. ✏️ around 1 🖐 on brown paper.

16. ✏️ around 1 🖐 on white paper.

17. ✂️ them out.

From the Hands of a Child II © 1994 Fearon Teacher Aids

18. ⊟ the brown 🖐 onto the white 🖐

leaving about 1/2" (1.3 cm) of the white

fingers showing.

19. ⊟ them to the side of the bag for a tail.

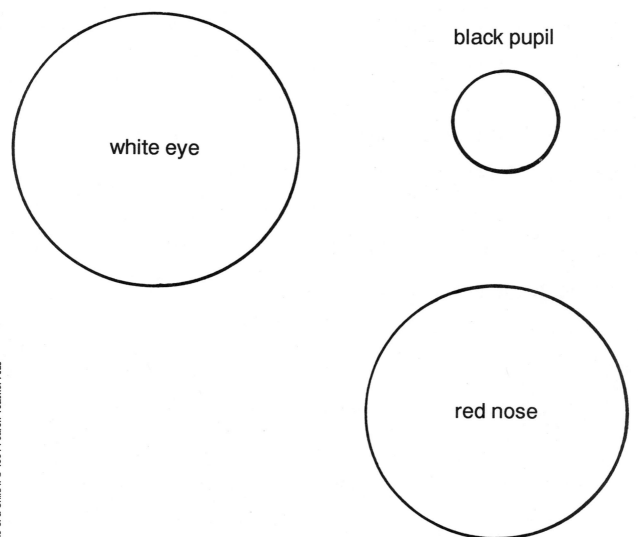

Christmas Angel _____

1. Stuff a ⬜ with scrap paper or crumpled newspaper.

2. Staple it closed across the top. 🛍

3. ✏️ around 2 🖐 🖐 on white paper.

4. ✂️ them out.

5. 🧴 1 🖐 to each side of the stuffed bag to make wings.

6. ✏️ the ⚪ on pink or brown paper.

7. ✂️ it out.

8. 🧴 the ⚪ to the top of the stuffed bag.

9. ✏️ the ⬓ on yellow, brown, or black paper.

10. ✂️ it out.

11. 🧴 the ⬓ around the ⚪ .

12. ✏️ features on the face.

13. ✏️ the ▭ on green paper.

14. ✂️ it out and fold it in half.

15. ✏️ 2 👍 👍 on pink or brown paper.

16. ✂️ them out.

17. 🧴 the 👍 👍 on each side of the 📖 .

18. 🧴 the 📖 to the center front of the stuffed bag.

From the Hands of a Child II © 1994 Fearon Teacher Aids

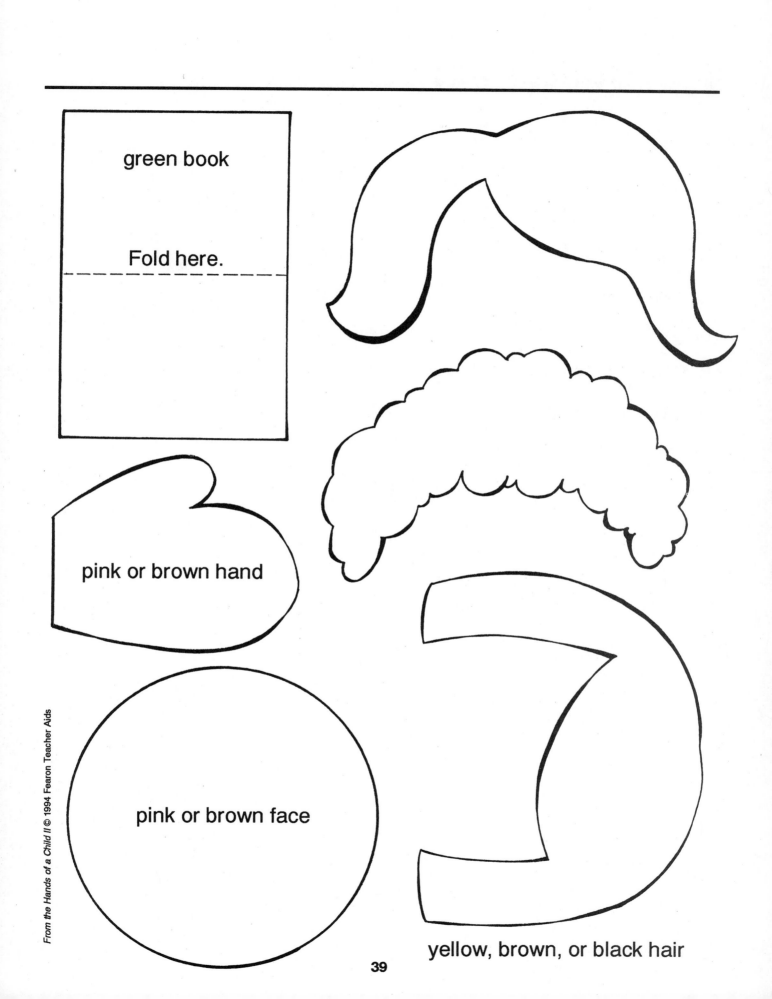

green book

Fold here.

pink or brown hand

pink or brown face

yellow, brown, or black hair

The Perfect Gift

1. ✏️ around many ✋ on green paper.

2. ✂️ them out.

3. Curl the fingers on each ✋.

4. Ask your teacher to staple the ✋ to the bulletin board to create a Christmas tree.

5. ✏️ a gift on white paper.

6. Color your gift with markers or crayons.

7. ✂️ out the gift and ask your teacher to staple it to the bulletin board.

From the Hands of a Child II © 1994 Fearon Teacher Aids

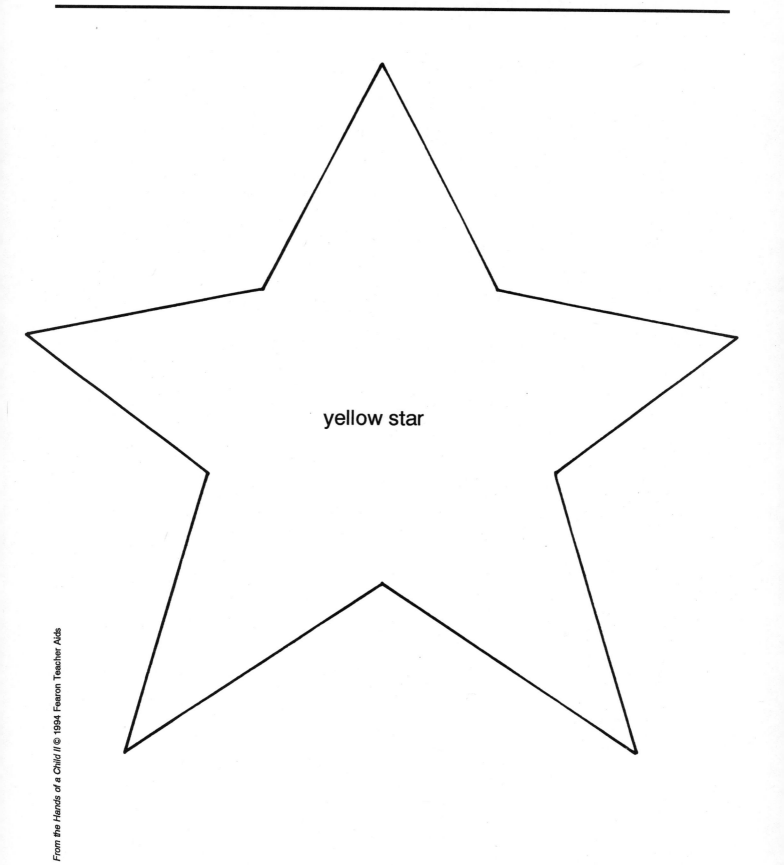

yellow star

January

Penguin

Materials for each child:
- orange, black, and yellow construction paper
- lunch bag (white)
- scrap paper or crumpled newspaper
- stapler
- paper plate
- pattern page
- scissors and paste

Read *Mr. Popper's Penguins* by Richard Atwater to the class before beginning this project. Discuss a penguin's living environment and other unique features of this bird.

Chinese Dragon

Materials for each child:
- orange, purple, yellow, red, blue, and green construction paper
- black marker
- pattern page
- scissors and paste

Discuss some of the customs of Chinese New Year before beginning the project. Read *Lion Dancer: Ernie Wan's Chinese New Year* by Kate Waters.

Snowman

Materials for each child:
- white, black, and red construction paper
- markers or crayons
- ruler
- pattern page
- scissors and paste

Invite children to make a list of signs that winter is approaching. Encourage children to discuss what winter activities they can do in the snow and what type of clothing is appropriate for outdoor winter play.

A Winter Scene

Materials for each child:
- white, green, black, red, brown, yellow, orange, and blue construction paper
- markers or crayons
- scissors and paste

Cover a bulletin board with blue butcher paper. Add a simple snowflake border. Cut out letters to make the display heading **A Winter Scene.** Glue children's hand tracings in rows to create snowy hills. Staple other winter pictures children make to the board.

Once this bulletin board is completed, use it as a story starter for creative writing.

Penguin

1. Stuff a ⬜ with scrap paper or crumpled newspaper.

2. Staple it closed across the top. 🛍️

3. ✏️ around 4 🖐️ 🖐️ 🖐️ 🖐️ on black paper.

4. ✂️ them out.

5. 🧴 1 ✋ to each side of the stuffed bag to make wings.

6. 🧴 2 ✋ ✋ to the bottom of the stuffed paper bag to make feet.

7. ✂️ out the ⬭ ▽ ∘∘ ○○ .

8. ✏️ the ⬭ on black paper.

9. ✂️ it out.

10. ✏️ the ▽ on orange paper.

11. ✂️ it out.

12. ✏️ 2 ○○ on yellow paper.

13. ✂️ them out.

14. ✏️ 2 ∘∘ on black paper.

15. ✂️ them out.

16. 🧴 the ●● to the center of the ○○ .

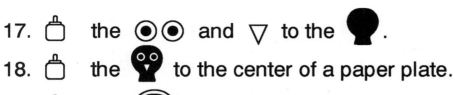

17. 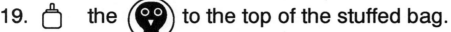 the ⊙⊙ and ▽ to the ♟.

18. the 🦉 to the center of a paper plate.

19. the 🦉 to the top of the stuffed bag.

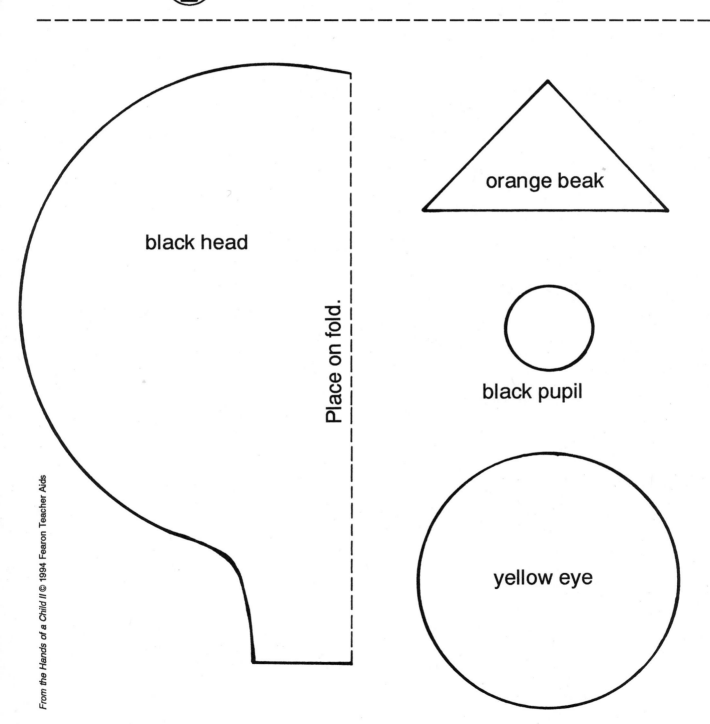

black head

Place on fold.

orange beak

black pupil

yellow eye

Chinese Dragon _____

1. ✂ out the ○○ ◁ ♀ ▭ .

2. ✏ the ♀ on green paper.

3. ✂ it out.

4. ✏ 2 ○○ on yellow paper.

5. ✂ them out.

6. 🖊 the ○○ onto the ♀ .

7. ✏ a pupil in the center of each eye

   using a black marker.

8. ✏ around 1 ✋ on orange paper.

9. ✂ it out.

10. 🖊 it to the end of the 👁 .

11. ✏ nostrils on the 👁 .

12. ✏ 2 ▭ ▭ on five colors of

    paper. Make 2 of each color.

13. ✂ them out.

14. Make a chain alternating colors. ⟨⬭⬭⬭⬭⬭⟩

15. 🖊 the 👁 to the ⟨⬭⬭⬭⬭⟩ .

16. ✏ the ◁ on orange paper.

17. ✂ it out.

18. 🖊 the ◁ to the end of the ⟨⬭⬭⬭⬭⬭⟩ .

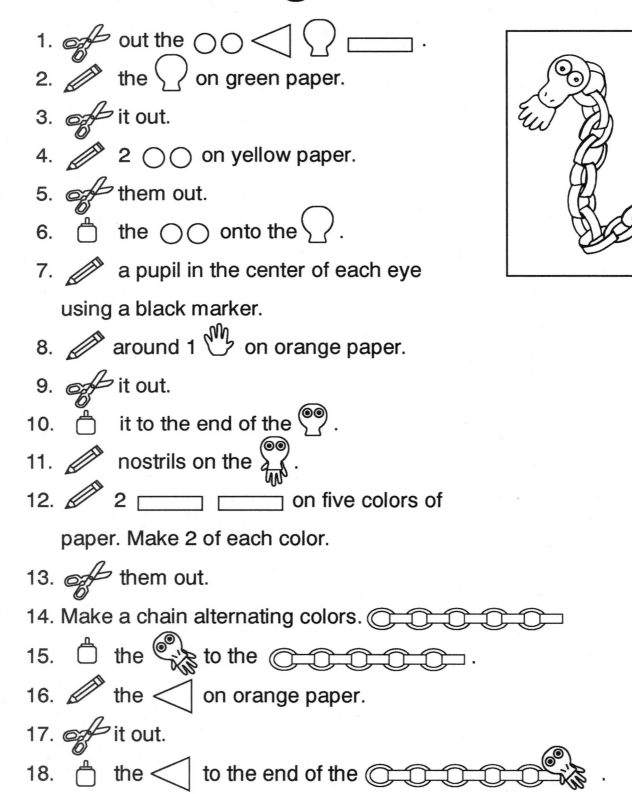

From the Hands of a Child II © 1994 Fearon Teacher Aids

body ring

green head

orange tail

yellow eye

Snowman

1. Fold a 9" x 12" (22.9 cm x 30.5 cm) sheet of white construction paper in half.

2. Draw a line across the open edge 1 1/2" (3.9 cm) from the top.

3. Draw lines 1" (2.5 cm) apart from the folded edge up to the pencil line.

4. ✂ the lines from the fold up to the pencil line.

5. Unfold and roll into a cylinder shape.

6. 🖊 edges in place.

7. ✏ around 2 ✋ ✋ on red paper.

8. ✂ them out.

9. 🖊 1 ✋ to each side of the top section of the lantern.

10. ✂ out the ◯ ○ ∘ ⬭ ⬛.

11. ✏ 2 ⬭ ⬭ on black paper.

12. ✂ them out.

13. Fold back 1/2" (1.3 cm) of the flat end of each foot.

14. 🖊 each ● to the inside bottom of the lantern.

From the Hands of a Child II © 1994 Fearon Teacher Aids

15. ✏️ the ◯ on white paper.

16. ✂️ it out.

17. ✏️ the ⬓ on black paper.

18. ✂️ it out.

19. 🖊 the ⬛ to the top of the ◯ .

20. ✏️ 2 ○ ○ on black paper.

21. ✂️ them out.

22. 🖊 • • to the ◡ .

23. ✏️ a mouth on the face.

24. ✏️ 2 ◯ ◯ on red paper.

25. ✂️ them out.

26. 🖊 ◯ ◯ to the front of the lantern.

black eye

black hat

black feet

white face

red button

Place on fold.

From the Hands of a Child II © 1994 Fearon Teacher Aids

A Winter Scene

1. ✏️ around many 🖐️ on white paper.

2. ✂️ them out.

3. Ask your teacher to staple the 🖐️ to the bulletin board to make snowy hills.

4. Create trees, buildings, a train, animals, or people from construction paper.

5. Ask your teacher to staple your creations to the winter scene bulletin board.

A WINTER SCENE

February

Stuffed Heart

Materials for each child:
- red or white butcher paper
- paper scraps or crumpled newspaper
- pink construction paper
- markers or crayons
- pattern page
- scissors and paste

This project provides the opportunity to discuss congruency because it is necessary to cut two heart shapes exactly the same size.

After children write kind words on their hearts, invite them to read the positive messages aloud to the class.

Cylinder Lincoln

Materials for each child:
- pink and black construction paper
- markers or crayons
- pattern page
- scissors and paste

Read about Abraham Lincoln to the class and encourage discussion about who he was and what he accomplished. Discuss the Gettysburg Address and Mr. Lincoln's top hat.

Washington Sculpture

Materials for each child:
- white construction paper
- paper bag
- scrap paper or crumpled newspaper
- stapler
- markers and crayons
- scissors and paste

Ask children whose picture is on a one-dollar bill. Ask children who George Washington was and what he did. Challenge children to consider what their lives might have been like if they had lived when George Washington was the President.

This is a good lesson to use to teach portrait drawing. Display a picture of George Washington for children to reference.

Special February People

Materials for each child:
- red butcher paper
- white construction paper
- markers or crayons
- pattern page
- scissors and paste

Cover a bulletin board with white butcher paper. Add a simple red border. Cut out letters to make the display heading **Special February People.** Enlarge the heart on page 55 to at least 18" (45.7 cm) and give each child a pattern. After children finish their projects, staple them to the board. Invite children to write an essay about their special person and share it orally.

Stuffed Heart

1. ✂ out the ♡.
2. ✏ 2 ♡ ♡ on red or white paper.
3. ✂ them out.
4. 🖊 around the edge of 1 ♡ about 1/4" (6 mm) from the edge. Do not glue a 6" (15. 2 cm) section on one side of the ♡.
5. Place the other ♡ on top. Allow the glue to dry.
6. Stuff the ♡ with paper scraps or crumpled newspaper.
7. 🖊 the hole closed.
8. ✏ around many 🖐 on pink paper.
9. ✂ them out.
10. 🖊 the 🖐 around the edge of the ♡.
11. Write kind words on your heart.

From the Hands of a Child II © 1994 Fearon Teacher Aids

red heart

Cylinder Lincoln

1. Roll a 9" x 12" (22.9 cm x 30.5 cm) black ☐ into a ⬭.

2. Overlap the edges 1 1/2" (3.9 cm) and 🖊 in place.

3. ✂ out the ⬤ ⌂ ◿ ▭.

4. ✏ 2 ◿ ◺ on pink paper.

5. ✂ them out.

6. ✏ 2 ▭ ▭ on black paper.

7. ✂ them out.

8. 🖊 1 ◺ to each ▬.

9. 🖊 1 ▬◿ to each side of the cylinder.

10. ✏ the ◯ on pink paper.

11. ✂ it out.

12. ✏ the ⌂ on black paper.

13. ✂ it out.

14. 🖊 the ⌂ to the ◯.

15. ✏ around 1 🖐 on black paper.

16. ✂ it out and curl the fingers.

17. 🖊 the 🖐 to the bottom edge of the ◯ to make a beard.

From the Hands of a Child II © 1994 Fearon Teacher Aids

18. ✏️ features and sideburns using markers or crayons.

19. 🫙 the 🎩 to the top of the cylinder.

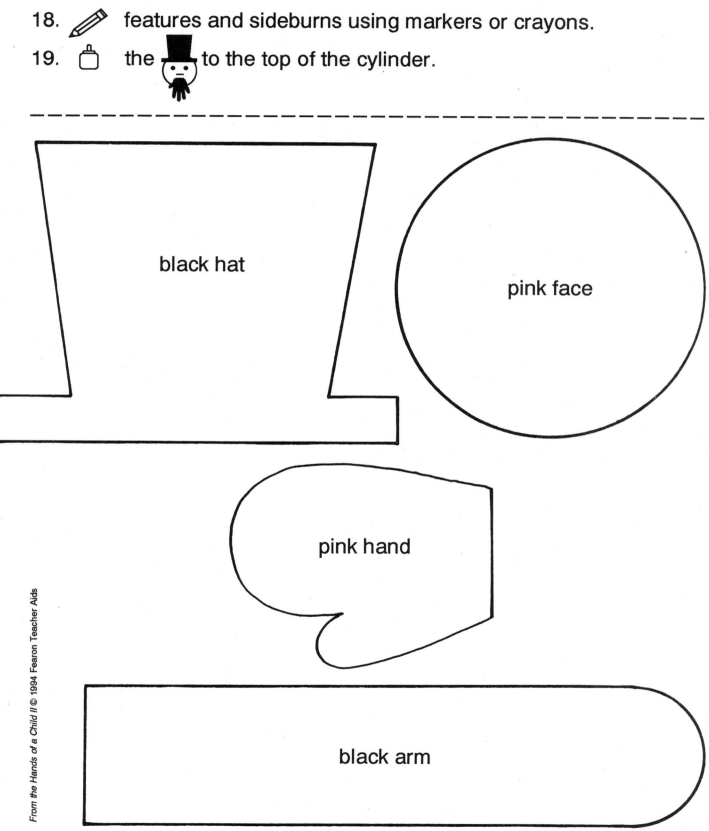

black hat

pink face

pink hand

black arm

Washington Sculpture _____

1. Stuff a  with scrap paper or crumpled newspaper.

2. Staple it closed across the top.

3. ✏ around many 🖐 on white paper.

4. ✂ them out.

5. 🖌 some of the 🖐 to the stuffed bag to make hair. Curl the fingers.

6. 🖌 the other 🖐 to the bottom of the stuffed bag to make a collar.

7. ✏ a face on the sculpture using the feature patterns on page 96.

From the Hands of a Child II © 1994 Fearon Teacher Aids

Special February People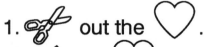_____

1. ✂ out the ♡.

2. ✎ the ♡ on red paper.

3. ✂ it out.

4. ✎ around many ✋ on white paper.

5. 🖊 the ✋ around the edge of the ♡.

6. ✎ a picture of a special February person,

   such as Martin Luther King, Jr.,

   Susan B. Anthony, Abraham Lincoln, or

   George Washington on white paper.

7. ✂ it out.

8. 🖊 the picture to the .

9. Ask your teacher to staple your ♡ to the

   bulletin board.

March

Lion

Materials for each child:
- orange, yellow, and white construction paper
- markers or crayons
- pattern page
- scissors and paste

Duplicate the cube on page 63 on orange paper for each child. Ask the children what they think the saying, "March comes in like a lion and out like a lamb" means.

Butterfly

Materials for each child:
- orange, pink, yellow, and white construction paper
- markers or crayons
- pattern page
- scissors and paste

Help children see the symmetry in their completed butterflies. Discuss the life cycle of a butterfly.

Leprechaun

Materials for each child:
- brown, yellow, green, orange, and pink construction paper
- ruler
- markers or crayons
- pattern page
- scissors and paste

Open a discussion about various cultures and their traditions. Discuss some Irish symbols, such as shamrocks, leprechauns, and Blarney stones.

End of the Rainbow

Materials for each child:
- white, violet, indigo, blue, green, yellow, orange, and red construction paper
- markers or crayons
- scissors

Cover the top of a bulletin board with blue butcher paper and the bottom of the board with green butcher paper. Add a simple border. Cut out letters to make the display heading **End of the Rainbow.** Create mountains by crunching brown construction or tissue paper. Staple the hand tracings to the board to create a rainbow. Trace and cut out a pot of gold using the enlarged pattern on page 69. Place the pot of gold at the end of the rainbow. Place the items children wish for at the end of the rainbow. Encourage children to write essays explaining their wishes.

Lion

1. ✂ out the cube.

2. Fold on the dotted lines.

3. 🗴 the tabs to the sides of the cube.

4. ✂ out the 🐻 ◯ .

5. ✏ the 🐻 on yellow paper.

6. ✂ it out.

7. ✏ 2 ◯ ◯ on white paper.

8. ✂ them out.

9. ✏ a black ● on each ◯ .

10. 🗴 the ◉ ◉ onto the 🐻 .

11. 🗴 the cube onto the 👀 to make a nose.

12. ✏ a mouth on the face.

13. ✏ around many 🖐 on orange paper.

14. 🗴 the 🖐 around the 🦁 to make the lion's

    mane.

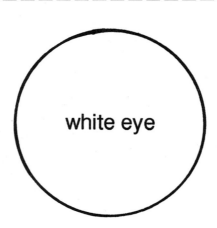

white eye

From the Hands of a Child II © 1994 Fearon Teacher Aids

yellow head

Place on fold.

Butterfly

1. Roll a 9" x 12" (22.9 cm x 30.5 cm) yellow [ ] into a ⬭ .

2. Overlap the edges so the tube is 1 1/2" (3.9 cm) wide.

3. 🖊 the edges in place.

4. ✏ 4 🖐 🖐 🖐 🖐 on yellow paper.

5. ✂ them out.

6. 🖊 2 🖐 🖐 to each side of the cylinder to make butterfly wings.

7. ✂ out the ○ ☐ ○ ▽ .

8. ✏ 2 ☐ ☐ and 2 ○ ○ on orange paper.

9. ✂ them out.

10. ✏ 2 ▽ ▽ on pink paper.

11. ✂ them out.

12. 🖊 the ☐ ☐ ○ ○ ▽ ▽ to the wings.

13. ✏ 2 ○ ○ on white paper.

14. ✂ them out.

15. ✏ a ● in each ○ .

16. 🖊 ◉ ◉ to the top of the cylinder.

17. ✏ a mouth below the eyes.

From the Hands of a Child II © 1994 Fearon Teacher Aids

orange square

orange circle

white eye

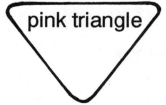

pink triangle

Leprechaun

1. Fold a 9" x 12" (22.9 cm x 30.5 cm) sheet of green construction paper in half.

2. Draw a line across the open edge 1 1/2" (3.9 cm) from the top.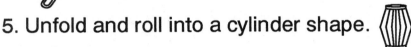

3. Draw lines 1" (2.5 cm) apart from the folded edge up to the pencil line.

4. ✂ the lines from fold up to the pencil line.

5. Unfold and roll into a cylinder shape.

6. 🖊 edges in place.

7. ✂ the ▭ ○ ⌷ ▯ ▱ ⌒ ⋈ .

8. ✏ 4 ▭ ▭ ▭ ▭ on green paper.

9. ✂ them out.

10. Accordion pleat each ▭ .

11. ✏ around 2 ✋ ✋ on pink or brown paper.

12. ✂ them out.

13. 🖊 the ✋ ✋ to the 〰 〰 .

14. ✏ 2 ⬚ on yellow paper.

15. ✂ them out.

16. 🖊 1 ⬚ to each 〰✋ .

17. 🖊 1 〰⬚✋ to each side of the top of the lantern.

18. ✏️ 2 ⬭ ⬭ on brown paper.

19. ✂️ them out.

20. 🖌️ the ⬭ ⬭ to the 〰️ 〰️ .

21. 🖌️ the 〰️ 〰️ to the bottom of the lantern.

22. ✏️ the ◯ on pink, or brown paper.

23. ✂️ it out.

24. ✏️ the ⌒ ⋈ on orange paper.

25. ✂️ them out.

26. 🖌️ the ⌒ to the top of the ◯ and the ⋈ to the

bottom.

27. ✏️ the 🎩 on green paper.

28. ✂️ it out.

29. 🖌️ the 🎩 to the top of the 🙂 .

30. ✏️ a face on the leprechaun using the feature

patterns on page 96.

- -

yellow cuff

orange bow tie

green hat

green arm and leg

brown shoe

pink or brown face

orange hair

From the Hands of a Child II © 1994 Fearon Teacher Aids

End of the Rainbow

1. ✏️ around 1 ✋ on violet, indigo, blue, green, yellow, orange, and red paper.

2. ✂️ them out.

3. Ask your teacher to staple the ✋ to the bulletin board to create a rainbow.

4. ✏️ what you would like to find at the end of the rainbow on white paper.

5. Color it and ✂️ it out.

6. Ask your teacher to place it at the end of the rainbow.

- -

yellow pot

April

Daffodil

Materials for each child:
- yellow, green, and blue construction paper
- pattern page
- scissors and paste

Encourage children to position the stem and long slender leaves in the center of the page. The stem should extend from the bottom of the flower down to the center of the bottom edge of the blue construction paper.

Baby Chick

Materials for each child:
- yellow, orange, and white construction paper
- markers or crayons
- pattern page
- scissors and paste

Begin a discussion about the new life of spring including baby chicks. Ask children where baby chicks come from and what they look like.

Cover a table with green paper and place the baby chicks on it. Encourage children to make larger cylinder chickens to place on the table with the baby chicks.

Rabbit and a Basket

Materials for each child:
- white, brown, green, yellow, pink, and purple construction paper
- markers or crayons
- pattern page
- scissors and paste

This project challenges the children to follow written and pictorial directions. Make sure the children trace their hands in a spread position.

April Showers Bring May Flowers

Materials for each child:
- red, yellow, white, green, and orange construction paper
- pattern page
- scissors and paste

Cover the top of a bulletin board with blue butcher paper and cover the bottom of the board with green butcher paper. Add a simple border. Cut out letters to make the display heading **April Showers Bring May Flowers.** Cut raindrops from white paper and add them to the board. Use children's colorful hand tracings to create an umbrella and flowers.

71

Daffodil

1. ✂ out the ✿ ▭ ▭◗ .

2. ✏ the ✿ on yellow paper.

3. ✂ it out.

4. ✏ around 1 ✋ on yellow paper.

5. ✂ it out and curl the fingers.

6. ✂ the bottom of the hand so it is straight.

7. Fold a tab about 1/2" (1.3 cm) wide at the base of the hand.

8. ✂ several slits on the folded tab.

9. 🖊 the tab of the ✋ to the center of the ✿ curving the tab slits inward so they form a circle. The fingers of the hand when standing upright should curve slightly outward.

10. 🖊 the ✲ to the top of a 9" x 12" (22.9 cm x 30.5 cm) sheet of blue paper.

11. ✏ 1 ▭ and 2 ▭◗ ▭◗ on green paper.

12. ✂ them out.

13. 🖊 the ⋎ to the blue paper below the ✲ .

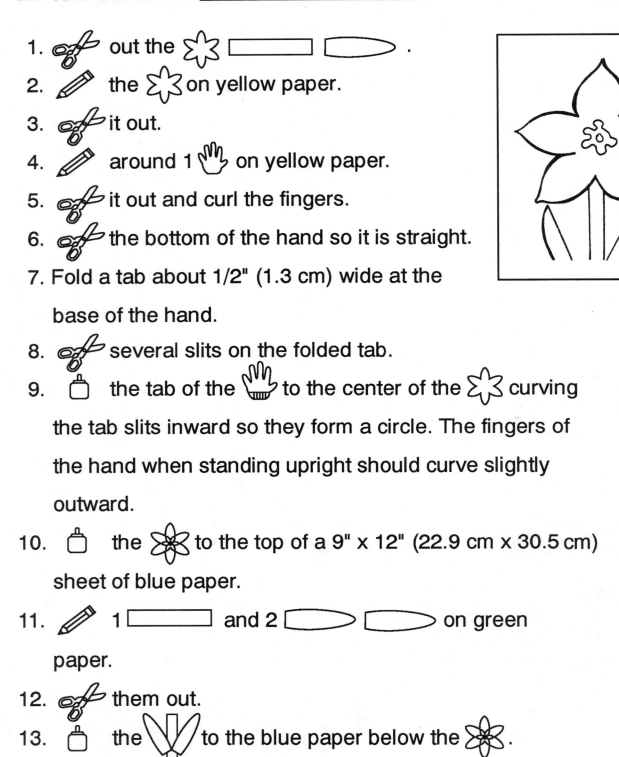

From the Hands of a Child II © 1994 Fearon Teacher Aids

yellow daffodil

green stem

green leaf

Baby Chick

1. Roll a 9" x 12" (22.9 cm x 30.5 cm) yellow ▭ into a ⬭ .

2. Overlap the edges 1 1/2" (3.9 cm) and ⬜ in place.

3. ✂ out the ◯ ◯ ▽ .

4. ✏ the ◯ on yellow paper.

5. ✂ it out.

6. ✏ 2 ◯ ◯ on white paper.

7. ✂ them out.

8. ⬜ the ◯ ◯ to the top half of the ◯ .

9. ✏ 2 ● ● on the ◯ ◯ .

10. ✏ the ▽ on orange paper.

11. ✂ it out.

12. ⬜ it to the ☺ .

13. ✏ around 2 🖐 🖐 on white paper.

14. ✂ them out.

15. ⬜ 1 🖐 to each side of the cylinder to make wings.

From the Hands of a Child II © 1994 Fearon Teacher Aids

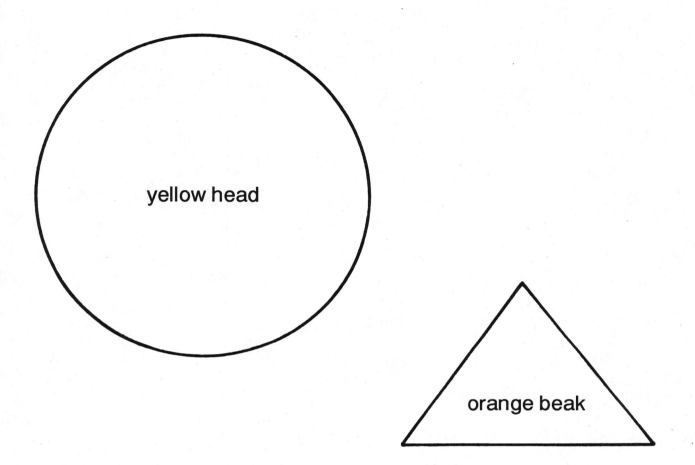

yellow head

orange beak

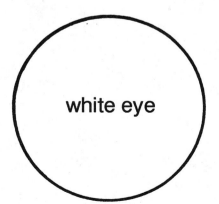

white eye

Rabbit and a Basket_____

1. Roll a 9" x 12" (22.9 cm x 30.5 cm) brown ▢ into a ⬭ .

2. Overlap the edges 1 1/2" (3.9 cm) and 🖊 in place.

3. ✏ around many 🖐 on green paper.

4. ✂ them out.

5. 🖊 some 🖐 around the inside of the cylinder at the top.

6. ✂ off the palm of the remaining 🖐 .

7. 🖊 them along the bottom of the outside of the cylinder to make grass.

8. ✂ a 1 1/2" x 12" (3.9 cm x 30.5 cm) strip of brown paper.

9. 🖊 the ▭ to the ⬭ to make a handle.

10. ✂ out the ◯ .

11. ✏ several ◯ on different colors of paper.

12. ✂ them out.

13. 🖊 the ◯ to the inside of the basket so most of the ◯ shows above the grass.

From the Hands of a Child II © 1994 Fearon Teacher Aids

14. ✏️ around 1 ✋ on white paper.

15. ✂️ it out.

16. Fold the middle finger under. 🖐️

17. Fold down the thumb and the pinky finger. ✌️

18. ✏️ a face on the bunny.

19. ✏️ paws on the bunny.

20. ✏️ the inside of the bunny's ears pink.

21. 🗒️ the bunny to the bottom of the basket.

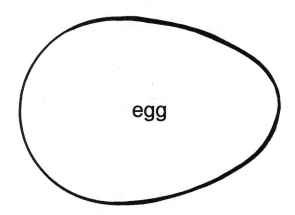

egg

April Showers Bring May Flowers

1. ✏️ around 6 🖐️🖐️🖐️🖐️🖐️🖐️ on yellow paper.

2. ✂️ them out.

3. Ask your teacher to staple them to the bulletin board to make an umbrella.

4. ✏️ around 1 🖐️ on any bright color of paper.

5. ✂️ it out.

6. ✂️ out the ▭ ⬭ .

7. ✏️ 1 ▭ and 2 ⬭ ⬭ on green paper.

8. ✂️ them out.

9. 🧴 1 ⬭ to each side of the ▭ .

10. 🧴 the 🌷 to the 🖐️ .

11. Ask your teacher to staple your flower to the bulletin board.

From the Hands of a Child II © 1994 Fearon Teacher Aids

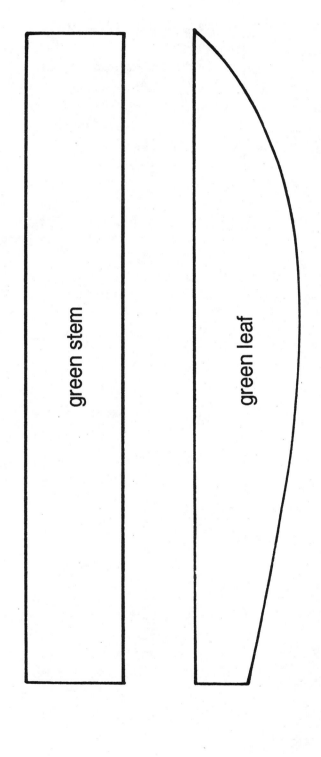

green stem

green leaf

May

Bouquet for Mom

Materials for each child:
- red, yellow, orange, pink, purple, and green construction paper
- popsicle sticks or bamboo skewers
- markers or crayons
- pattern page
- scissors and paste

Challenge children to consider ways they can be helpful at home as they create a helping-hands bouquet for Mother's Day.

Discuss congruency with the children as they glue identical hand tracings back to back to make flowers.

Frog

Materials for each child:
- black, green, and white construction paper
- paper bag
- scrap paper or crumpled newspaper
- stapler
- pattern page
- scissors and paste

Discuss where frogs might be found. Ask children to compare the metamorphosis of frogs and butterflies. Ask children what a frog looks like before it becomes a frog and what a butterfly is before it becomes a butterfly. You may want to make a bulletin-board display showing the life cycle of both creatures.

Clown

Materials for each child:
  - white, red, orange, black, and yellow construction paper
  - ruler
  - markers or crayons
  - pattern page
  - scissors and paste

Ask children to tell about experiences they have had at a circus. Discuss circus clowns and what makes them special. Discuss laughter and its importance in our lives.

Our Flag

Materials for each child:
  - red, white, and blue construction paper
  - markers or crayons
  - pattern page
  - scissors and paste

Cover a bulletin board with white butcher paper to make a huge flag. Outline thirteen stripes and a section (seven stripes long) for the field of stars. Cut out letters to make the display heading **Many People Built Our Flag.** Divide the class into three groups for making hand tracings—red group, blue group, and white group. Glue red hand tracings on every other stripe beginning with the first stripe at the top. Glue the white hand tracings on the alternate stripes. Glue the blue hand tracings to the field of stars. Add fifty white stars to the blue field. Add the pictures children draw of famous Americans along the bottom of the flag.

Bouquet for Mom _____

1. ✏️ around 2 ✋🤚 on red, yellow, orange, pink, and purple paper. Make 2 🤚✋ of each color.

2. ✂️ them out.

3. 🖌️ a popsicle stick that has been painted green between each pair of 🤚.

4. ✂️ out the ⬛️▭.

5. ✏️ 10 ▭ ▭ ▭ ▭ ▭
   ▭ ▭ ▭ ▭ ▭
   on green paper.

6. ✂️ them out.

7. 🖌️ 2 ▭ ▭ to each ✋.

8. ✏️ a message on each flower that would make your mother happy, such as "Good for one hug" or "Good for cleaning my room cheerfully."

9. ✏️ 2 ⬛️ ⬛️ on red paper.

10. ✂️ them out.

11. 🖌️ the edges of the ⬛️ together leaving the top open.

12. Place your 🌷 in the ⬛️.

From the Hands of a Child II © 1994 Fearon Teacher Aids

red vase

green leaf

Frog

1. Stuff a  with scrap paper or crumpled newspaper.

2. Staple it closed across the top.

3. ✏ around 4 🖐🖐🖐🖐 on green paper.

4. ✂ them out.

5. 🧴 1 🖐 to each side of the stuffed bag to make hands.

6. 🧴 2 🖐 🖐 to the bottom of the paper bag for feet.

7. ✂ out the ⬭ ○ ₒ .

8. ✏ 2 ○○ on white paper.

9. ✂ them out.

10. ✏ 2 ₒ ₒ on black paper.

11. ✂ them out.

12. 🧴 the ● ● to the ○○ .

13. ✏ the ⬭ on green paper.

14. ✂ it out.

15. 🧴 the ◉◉ to the ⬭ so that the ◉◉ stick up above the straight edge of the face.

16. 🧴 the ◉◉ to the top of the paper bag.

From the Hands of a Child II © 1994 Fearon Teacher Aids

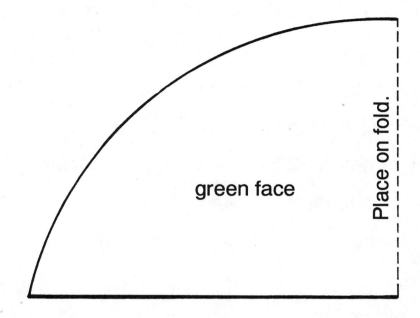

green face

Place on fold.

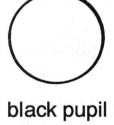

black pupil

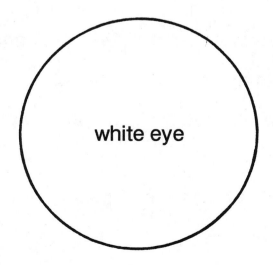

white eye

Clown

1. Fold a 9" x 12" (22.9 cm x 30.5 cm) sheet of white construction paper in half.

2. Draw a line across the open edge 1 1/2" (3.9 cm) from the top.

3. Draw lines 1" (2.5 cm) apart from the folded edge up to the pencil line.

4. ✂ the lines from the fold up to the pencil line.

5. Unfold and roll into a cylinder shape.

6. ⌸ edges in place.

7. ✏ around many 🖐 on yellow paper.

8. ✂ them out.

9. Bend up 1/2" (1.3 cm) of the palm end of each hand to make a tab.

10. ⌸ the tab of each 👆 to the bottom inside section of the lantern to make the clown's collar.

11. ✏ around 2 🖐 🖐 on orange paper.

12. ✂ them out.

13. ⌸ 1 🖐 to the top of each side of the lantern to make the clown's hair.

From the Hands of a Child II © 1994 Fearon Teacher Aids

14. ✂ out the ◯ ⌣ △ ⌂ .

15. ✏ the ◯ ⌣ on red paper.

16. ✂ them out.

17. 🔖 them to the lantern to make the nose and

mouth.

18. ✏ a line on the ⌣ with a black marker.

19. ✏ 2 ⌒ ⌒ on white paper.

20. ✂ them out.

21. ✏ a • inside each ⌒ .

22. 🔖 the ⦿ ⦿ above the nose on the lantern.

23. ✏ the ⌂ on a folded piece of black paper.

24. ✂ it out.

25. 🔖 the ⬛ to the lantern.

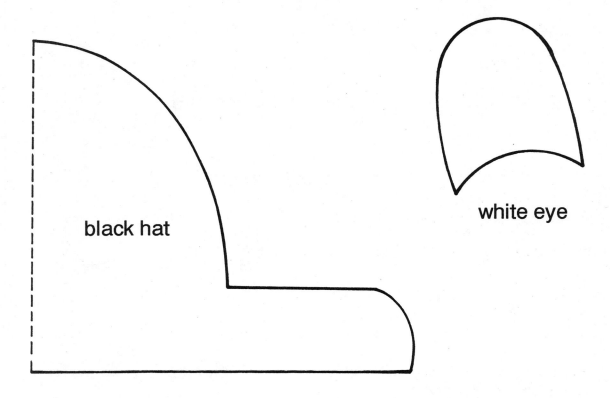

black hat

white eye

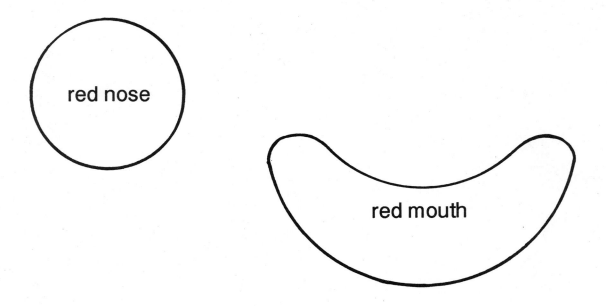

red nose

red mouth

Our Flag _____

1. 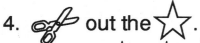 around many  on red, white, or blue paper.

2. ✂ them out.

3. Ask your teacher to staple them to the bulletin board.

4. ✂ out the ☆.

5. ✏ 2 ☆ ☆ on white paper.

6. ✂ them out.

7. Ask your teacher to staple the ☆ to the blue section of the bulletin board until there are 50.

8. ✏ a famous American, such as a war hero, President of the United States, or other person who has helped make our country what it is today, on a sheet of white paper.

9. ✂ it out.

10. Ask your teacher to staple it to the bulletin board.

- -

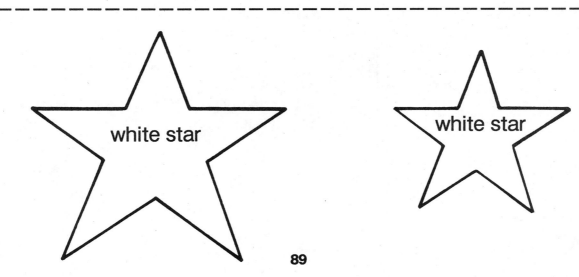

white star

white star

June

Summer Sun

Materials for each child:
- orange, yellow, and black construction paper
- markers or crayons
- pattern page
- scissors and paste

As children make their projects, challenge them to think about ways the sun helps us and ways it can be damaging. Encourage children to think about ways they can protect themselves from overexposure to the sun's rays.

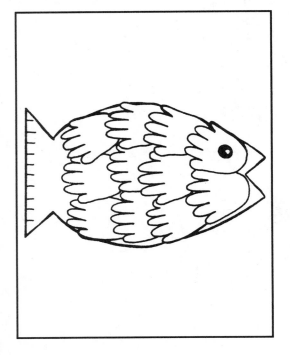

Stuffed Fish

Materials for each child:
- orange or white butcher paper
- orange and black construction paper
- paper scraps or crumpled newspaper
- black marker
- pattern page
- scissors and paste

This is a good project to use at the end of the year to get rid of old scraps of paper.

Encourage children to discuss fun summer recreational activities, such as fishing.

Summer's On Its Way

Materials for each child:
- blue paper
- 9" (22.9 cm) squares of white paper
- markers or crayons
- scissors and paste

Cover a bulletin board with white butcher paper. Cut out letters to make the display heading **Summer Fun.** Cut out a large yellow half circle for a sun and staple in place. Divide the class into three groups. Give each group a different color of blue paper to make hand tracings. Place the blue hand tracings along the bottom of the board to make ocean waves. Staple orange hand tracings along the edge of the sun. Staple the boats along the waves.

Summer Sun

1. ✂ out the ◯ 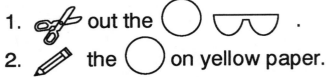 .
2. ✏ the ◯ on yellow paper.
3. ✂ it out.
4. ✏ around many ✋ on orange paper.
5. ✂ them out.
6. 🖊 the ✋ all the way around the edge of the ◯ .
7. ✏ the ⌒⌒ on black paper.
8. ✂ it out.
9. 🖊 the 🕶 to the ☀ .
10. ✏ a mouth on your sun.

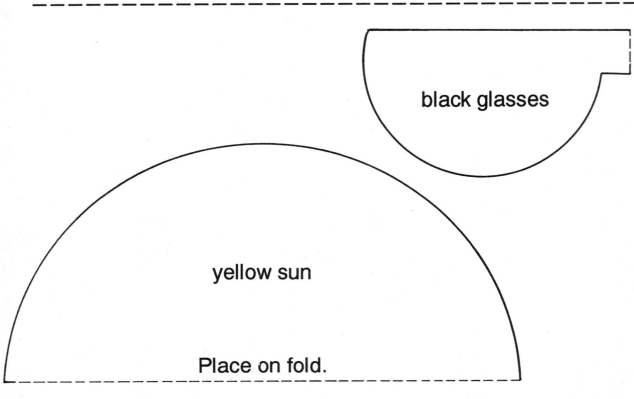

black glasses

Place on fold.

yellow sun

Place on fold.

From the Hands of a Child II © 1994 Fearon Teacher Aids

Stuffed Fish

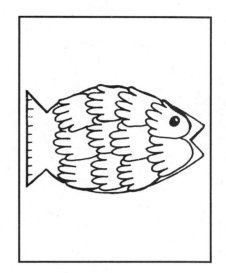

1. ✂ out the 🐟 ◯ .

2. ✏ 2 🐟 🐟 on orange or white paper.

3. ✂ them out.

4. 🖊 the edge of 1 🐟 leaving a 4" (10.2 cm) section unglued.

5. Place the other 🐟 on top.

6. ✏ around many 🖐 on orange paper.

7. ✂ them out and curl the fingers.

8. 🖊 the 🖐 to both sides of the 🐟 beginning at the tail and working toward the head. Trim away the 🖐 that overlap the mouth.

9. ✏ 2 ◯ ◯ on black paper.

10. ✂ them out.

11. 🖊 1 ● to each side of the 🐟 .

12. Stuff the fish with paper scraps or crumpled newspaper.

13. 🖊 the opening closed.

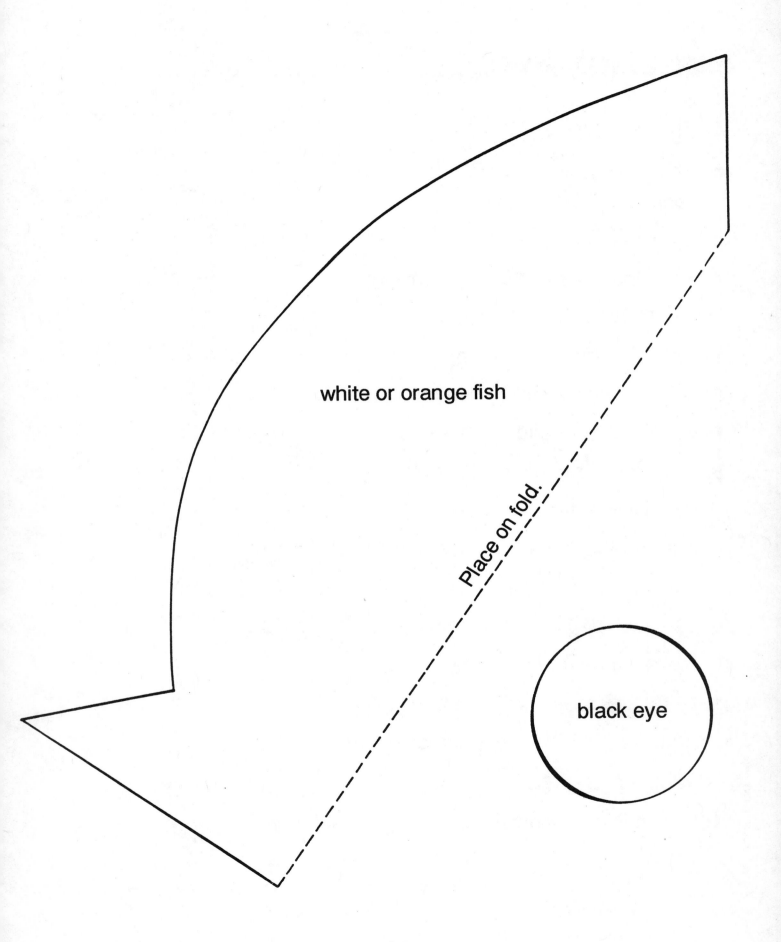

white or orange fish

Place on fold.

black eye

Summer's On Its Way

1. ✏️ around many ✋ on blue paper.
2. ✂️ them out.
3. Ask your teacher to staple them to the bulletin board to make ocean waves.
4. Fold a 9" (22.9 cm) square of white paper in half to make a ▽.
5. Fold the folded edge up about 1 1/2" (3.9 cm) to make a cuff.
6. ✏️ people in your boat.
7. Ask your teacher to staple your boat to the bulletin board.

Feature Patterns_____

Eyes

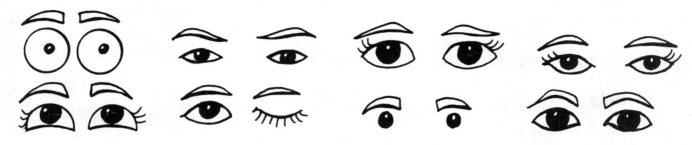

Noses

Mouths

Ears